Why I
Love

Christmas

by Michael Wagner
illustrated by
Tom Jellett

PUFFIN BOOKS

I love Christmas because it brings everyone together. There are so many lovely traditions that help us bond more closely as family and friends. We also give and receive gifts, share food and sing songs. It's a special time of year that brings out the kindness in us all.

For Maisy Moo and Ollie Sue – MICHAEL

I love Christmas because if there's too much food on the day, you can eat the rest on Boxing Day. On sandwiches! That is my most favourite sandwich of the year. I don't really know why they call it Boxing Day. Something about donation boxes and giving boxes of gifts to people in need. Which sounds like a great thing to do on Boxing Day. And sandwiches.

For Darby, Billy, and Eddie – TOM

PUFFIN BOOKS

UK | USA | Canada | Ireland | Australia | India | New Zealand | South Africa | China

Penguin Random House Australia

Penguin Random House Australia is part of the Penguin Random House group of companies whose addresses can be found at global.penguinrandomhouse.com.

First published by Puffin Books, an imprint of Penguin Random House Australia Pty Ltd, in 2024

Design by Tony Palmer and Tom Jellett © Penguin Random House Australia Pty Ltd
Printed in China

Penguin Random House Australia uses papers that are natural and recyclable products, made from wood grown in sustainable forests. The logging and manufacture processes are expected to conform to the environmental regulations of the country of origin.

ISBN 978 1 76134468 8

penguin.com.au

We acknowledge that Aboriginal and Torres Strait Islander peoples are the Traditional Custodians and the first storytellers of the lands on which we live and work. We honour Aboriginal and Torres Strait Islander peoples' continuous connection to Country, waters, skies and communities. We celebrate Aboriginal and Torres Strait Islander stories, traditions and living cultures; and we pay our respects to Elders past and present.

Do you know what the BEST time of the WHOLE YEAR is?

I do. It's easy.

I love it SO SO SO SO much.

And here's why . . .

The whole thing begins when you get your advent calendar.

Then, decorations start popping up all over the place.
Christmas songs are EVERYWHERE . . .

and who cares how hot it is,
there has to be snow!

Things REALLY get exciting when you decorate your Christmas tree . . .

and when you put LOTS of lights up around the house.

Then comes the . . .

STREET PARTY!

We have one every year.

They don't let cars in,
so you can play EVERYWHERE!

And ours isn't the only street
that celebrates Christmas.

That's the best one yet.
Isn't it fabulous?!

In our family, all the cousins make gingerbread houses together.

And we always make
cards and bake presents.

At Christmas,
even shopping is fun!

Some kids aren't as lucky as us
so we get them something too.

And as soon as the school holidays start,
all sorts of amazing things happen!

There's singing at the park . . .
and even fireworks!

Then, all of a sudden, you're down to the last window on your advent calendar.

And there's only one more sleep to go!

Dad says if you go to bed early, Christmas Day comes sooner . . .
I'm too excited to sleep, Dad.
Just pretend tomorrow's an ordinary day.
But HOW, Dad?

IT'S CHRISTMAS DAY!!!

MERRY CHRISTMAS!

MERRY CHRISTMAS!!
Let's give our presents out one at a time ... no gift frenzy!

As soon as Mum and Dad
are properly awake,
we hand out the presents.

And that's AWESOME, but then
it's time for my VERY, VERY favourite
part of the day . . .

Christmas lunch at Nanna's!
Everyone brings
something tasty to eat.

Would you mind carving, Ben? That was always Grandpa's job.
Of course.
Grandpa loved Christmas Day as much as me. We miss him A LOT.

Before dessert, we have speeches.

Dad always remembers to say
the important things . . .

Christmas Day is the happiest, kindest, nicest, most fun day of the whole year.

And then, far too soon . . .

. . . it's time to go home,

feeling full and happy and tired and glad.

That's why I love Christmas
SO SO SO SO MUCH.

And, guess what?

It's coming again soon!

I can't wait! Can you?